Your Friendship Is a Gift from God

Paintings by
DEB STRAIN

HARVEST HOUSE PUBLISHERS
EUGENE, OREGON

Your Friendship Is a Gift from God

For My Friend:

Sandra

With Love,

Allegra

If, out of time, I could pick a moment
And keep it shining, always new,
Of all the days that I have lived,
I'd pick the moment I met you.

AUTHOR UNKNOWN

SAGE

©Deb Strain

Friendship improves
happiness and abates
misery, by the doubling
of our joy and the dividing
of our grief

MARCUS TULLIUS CICERO

A true friend warms
you by her presence,
trusts you with her
secrets, remembers
you in her prayers.

AUTHOR UNKNOWN

A friend loves at all times.

THE BOOK OF PROVERBS

I love the time I spend with you,
   because you're one of those friends
   I always have a good time with.
Even when I'm feeling down,
   you manage to help me feel better about things.
You really listen,
   and it's obvious you care.
I appreciate your positive attitude
   and the fact that no matter what I do,
   you always see the best in me.
There's not a doubt in my mind
   why God put you in my life…
He wanted me to know what
   a real friend is.

LINDA L. ELROD

Fox Glove • Thyme • Parsley •

Heather

Sorrel •

Marjoram •

Rosem...

*Perfume and incense bring
joy to the heart, and the
pleasantness of one's
friend springs from his
earnest counsel.*

THE BOOK OF PROVERBS

True friendship
comes when silence
between two people
is comfortable.

DAVE TYSON GENTRY

9

The secret to friendship is being a good listener.

AUTHOR UNKNOWN

Friendship is the union of spirits, a marriage of hearts, and the bond thereof virtue.

WILLIAM PENN

Friendship is a horizon—which expands whenever we approach it.

E. R. HAZLIP

Beeskeep Garden

Life's Sweetest Joys Are Those Shared With A Friend♥

Good friends must not always be together. It is the feeling of oneness when distant that proves a lasting friendship.

SUSAN P. SCHULTZ

Friendship is the
inexpressible comfort
of feeling safe with a
person, having neither
to weigh thoughts nor
measure words.

GEORGE ELIOT

See God in every person, place, and thing, and all will be well in your world.

LOUISE HAY

Great and numerous as are the blessings of friendship, this certainly is the sovereign one, that it gives us bright hopes for the future and forbids weakness and despair. In the face of a true friend a man sees as it were a second self. So that where his friend is he is; if his friend be rich, he is not poor; though he be weak, his friend's strength is his; and in his friend's life he enjoys a second life after his own is finished.

MARCUS CICERO

©Deb Strain

*Every good and perfect
gift is from above, coming
down from the Father of
the heavenly lights.*

THE BOOK OF JAMES

Friends are like windows
through which you see out
into the world and back into
yourself...If you don't have
friends, you see much less
than you otherwise might.

MERLE SHAIN

Friends are God's way of taking care of us.

AUTHOR UNKNOWN

My Heart ♥ is in the

Garden

©Deb Strain

If we would build on a sure foundation in friendship, we must love friends for their sake rather than for our own.

CHARLOTTE BRONTË

Love
one another
deeply,
from the heart.

THE BOOK OF 1 PETER

19

Some Friends Are Forever

Sometimes in life,
you find a special friend;
someone who changes your life
by being a part of it.

Someone who makes you laugh
until you can't stop;
someone who makes you believe
that there really is good in this world.

Someone who convinces you
that there is an unlocked door
just waiting for you to open it.

This is forever friendship.

When you're down,
and the world seems dark and empty,
your forever friend lifts you up in spirit
and makes that dark and empty world
suddenly seem dark and full.

Your forever friend gets you through
the hard times, and the sad times,
and the confused times.
If you turn and walk away
your forever friend follows.
If you lose your way,
your forever friend guides you
and cheers you on.

Your forever friend holds your hand
and tells you that
everything is going to be a-okay.

And when you find such a friend,
you'll feel happy and complete,
because you need not worry.

You have a forever friend for life
and forever has no end.

LAURIEANN KELLY

© Deb Strain

Friendship is one of the sweetest joys in life.

CHARLES SPURGEON

Among the great and glorious gifts
our heavenly Father sends
Is the gift of understanding
that we find in loving friends.

HELEN STEINER RICE

Good friends open their
ears and hearts more than
they open their mouths.

AUTHOR UNKNOWN

Good friends are
flowers that never fade.

AUTHOR UNKNOWN

Flexible people
don't get bent
out of shape.

AUTHOR UNKNOWN

There is no greater joy than giving joy away.
Because it comes back to you, in actual double pay;
You are the one who benefits from spreading joy and cheer
And yet it only takes a smile, to brush away a tear.
The joy we share within our hearts from day to day
Depicts the love of Jesus and His sweet loving way.
We cannot do for others and enjoy the great reward,
Unless we share with others the words of our dear Lord.

GRACE TAYLOR

24

© Deb Strain

At first as they stumped along the path which edged the Hundred
Acre Wood, they didn't say much to each other; but when they
came to the stream, and had helped each other across the stepping
stones, and were able to walk side by side again over the heather,
they began to talk in a friendly way about this and that.

A.A. MILNE
Winnie-the-Pooh

Wounds from a friend can be trusted.

THE BOOK OF PROVERBS

©Deb Strain

What can be more delightful than to have some one to whom you can say everything with the same absolute confidence as to yourself? Is not prosperity robbed of half its value if you have no one to share your joy? On the other hand, misfortunes would be hard to bear if there were not some one to feel them even more acutely than yourself.

MARCUS CICERO

A man of many companions may come to ruin,
but there is a friend who sticks closer than a brother.

THE BOOK OF PROVERBS

Dear friend, I pray thee, if thou wouldst be proving
Thy strong regard for me,
Make me no vows. Lip-service is not loving;
Let thy faith speak for thee.

ELLA WHEELER WILCOX

A true friendship is
as wise as it is tender.

HENRY DAVID THOREAU

Thyme

SaGe

Basil

DiLL

Chives

©Deb Strain

A female friend,
amiable, clever,
and devoted, is a
possession more
valuable than parks
and palaces.

LORD BEACONSFIELD

Lavender

A beloved friend does not fill
one part of the soul, but,
penetrating the whole, becomes
connected with all feeling.

WILLIAM ELLERY CHANNING

A pure friendship inspires, cleanses, expands, and strengthens the soul.

HORATIO ALGER

Dear friend, I pray that you may enjoy good health and that all may go well with you, even as your soul is getting along well.

THE BOOK OF 3 JOHN

A true friend is more precious to the soul than all which it inherits beneath the sun.

WASHINGTON IRVING

Be true to thy friend.

AUTHOR UNKNOWN

Friendship does not spring up and grow great and become perfect all at once, but requires time and the nourishment of thoughts.

DANTE

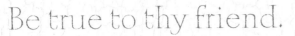

A principal fruit of friendship is the ease and discharge of the fullness and swelling of the heart, which passions of all kinds do cause and induce. No receipt openeth the heart but a true friend, to whom you may impart griefs, joys, fears, hopes, suspicions, counsels, and whatsoever lieth upon the heart to oppress it, in a kind of civil shrift or confession.

FRANCIS BACON

We talked of a future life, of art, service, marriage, and education; nor did the idea ever occur to us that very possibly all we said was shocking nonsense. The reason why it never occurred to us was that the nonsense which we talked was good, sensible nonsense, and that, so long as one is young, one can appreciate good nonsense, and believe in it. In youth the powers of the mind are directed wholly to the future, and that future assumes such various, vivid, and alluring forms under the influence of hope—hope based, not upon the experience of the past, but upon an assumed possibility of happiness to come—that such dreams of expected felicity constitute in themselves the true happiness of that period of our life.

LEO TOLSTOY

Love is all very well in its way, but friendship is much higher. Indeed, I know of nothing in the world that is either nobler or rarer than a devoted friendship.

OSCAR WILDE

©Deb Strain

Friends…they cherish each other's hopes.
They are kind to each other's dreams.

HENRY DAVID THOREAU

*If one falls down, his friend
can help him up. But pity
the man who falls and has
no one to help him up!
Also, if two lie down
together, they will keep
warm. But how can one
keep warm alone? Though
one may be overpowered,
two can defend themselves.
A cord of three strands is
not quickly broken.*

THE BOOK OF ECCLESIASTES

No friendship is an accident.

O HENRY

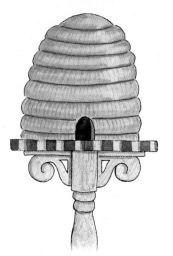

A true friend embraces
our objects as her own.
We feel another mind
bent on the same end,
enjoying it, ensuring it,
reflecting it, and delighting
in our devotion to it.

WILLIAM ELLERY CHANNING

They embarked upon an open and declared friendship.
They even talked about friendship. They went to the
Zoological Gardens together one Saturday to see for
themselves a point of morphological interest about the
toucan's bill—that friendly and entertaining bird—
and they spent the rest of the afternoon walking
about and elaborating in general terms this theme
and the superiority of intellectual fellowship to all
merely passionate relationships.

H.G. WELLS
Ann Veronica

A friend is a rare book of which only one copy is made.

AUTHOR UNKNOWN

By friendship you mean the greatest love, the greatest usefulness, the most open communication, the noblest sufferings, the severest truth, the heartiest counsel, and the greatest union of minds of which brave men and women are capable.

JEREMY TAYLOR

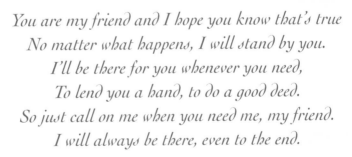

You are my friend and I hope you know that's true
No matter what happens, I will stand by you.
I'll be there for you whenever you need,
To lend you a hand, to do a good deed.
So just call on me when you need me, my friend.
I will always be there, even to the end.

AUTHOR UNKNOWN

It may be hard work sometimes, but a friend's
hand and voice make it easy.

ANNA SEWELL

*Don't flatter yourself that
friendship authorizes you to say
disagreeable things to your
intimates. The nearer you come
into relation with a person,
the more necessary do tact
and courtesy become.*

OLIVER WENDELL HOLMES

There is nothing better
than the encouragement
of a good friend.

KATHARINE BUTLER HATHAWAY

©Deb Strain

A good laugh makes us better friends with ourselves and everybody around us.

ORISON SWEET MARDEN